NERD CULTURE

NERDING OUT ABOUT

FANTASY

T0061999

VIRGINIA LOH-HAGAN

45TH PARALLEL PRESS

Published in the United States of America by Cherry Lake Publishing Group
Ann Arbor, Michigan
www.cherrylakepublishing.com

Reading Adviser: Beth Walker Gambro, MS, Ed., Reading Consultant, Yorkville, IL
Book Designer: Joseph Hatch

Photo Credits: © KissShot, Adobe Stock, cover, title page; © alexan888/Shutterstock, 4; © Andrei Diomidov/ Shutterstock, 7; © Stepan Kapl/Shutterstock, 8; Mårten Eskil Winge, Public domain, via Wikimedia Commons, 10; Viktor Vasnetsov, Public domain, via Wikimedia Commons, 12; © Christian Mueller/Shutterstock, 15; © TinoFotografie/Shutterstock, 16; Harris & Ewing, Public domain, via Wikimedia Commons, 19; © Photo Spirit/ Shutterstock, 21; © Moviestore Collection Ltd/Alamy Stock Photo, 22; © DFree/Shutterstock, 24; © Julia Zavalishina/Shutterstock, 26; © Ironika/Shutterstock, 29; © Prostock-studio/Shutterstock, 30

45th Parallel Press is an imprint of Cherry Lake Publishing Group.

Library of Congress Cataloging-in-Publication Data

Names: Loh-Hagan, Virginia, author.
Title: Nerding out about fantasy / Virginia Loh-Hagan.
Description: Ann Arbor, Michigan : 45th Parallel Press, 2024. | Series:
  Nerd culture | Audience: Grades 4-6. | Summary: "Nerding Out About
  Fantasy covers the wonderfully nerdy world of fantasy: from languages
  spoken in fantasy worlds to popular fantasy games. This 45th Parallel
  hi-lo series includes considerate vocabulary and high-interest
  content"-- Provided by publisher.
Identifiers: LCCN 2023035097 | ISBN 9781668939338 (paperback) | ISBN
  9781668938294 (hardcover) | ISBN 9781668940679 (ebook) | ISBN
  9781668942024 (pdf)
Subjects: LCSH: Fantasy fiction--History and criticism--Juvenile
  literature. | Fantasy games--Juvenile literature. | Fantasy--Juvenile
  literature. | LCGFT: Literary criticism.
Classification: LCC PN3435 .L55 2024 | DDC 809.3/8766--dc23/eng/20230830
LC record available at *https://lccn.loc.gov/2023035097*

Cherry Lake Publishing Group would like to acknowledge the work of the Partnership for 21st Century Learning, a Network of Battelle for Kids. Please visit Battelle for Kids online for more information.

Note from publisher: Websites change regularly, and their future contents are outside of our control. Supervise children when conducting any recommended online searches for extended learning opportunities.

Printed in the United States of America

Dr. Virginia Loh-Hagan is an author and educator. She is currently the Director of the Asian Pacific Islander Desi American (APIDA) Center at San Diego State University and the Co-Executive Director of The Asian American Education Project. She lives in San Diego with her very tall husband and very naughty dogs.

TABLE OF CONTENTS

Nerds are now trendy. More and more people become fantasy nerds every day!

LIVING THE NERDY LIFE

It's finally cool to be a nerd. Nerd culture is everywhere. It's in movies. It's on TV. It's in video games. It's in books. Everyone is talking about it. Everyone is watching it. Everyone is doing it. There's no escaping nerd culture.

Nerds and sports fans are alike. They have a lot in common. Instead of sports, nerds like nerdy things. Magic is nerdy. Science fiction is nerdy. Superheroes are nerdy. Nerds obsess over these interests. They're huge fans. They have a great love for a topic. They learn all they can. They spend hours on their hobbies. Hobbies are activities. Nerds hang with others who feel the same.

Nerds form **fandoms**. Fandoms are nerd networks. They're communities of fans. Nerds host online group chats. They host meetings. They host **conventions**. Conventions are large gatherings. They have speakers. They have workshops. They're also called **expos**. Tickets sell fast. Everyone wants to go. Nerd conventions are the place to be.

Nerd culture is on the rise. It's very popular. But it didn't used to be. Nerds used to be bullied. They were made fun of. They weren't seen as cool. They'd rather study than party. This made them seem odd. They were seen as different. Not anymore! Today, nerds rule!

Fantasy in real life! Fans of *The Lord of the Rings* books can visit a movie set that looks like the Shire. The Shire is where some Hobbits live in the story.

Fantasy is different from science fiction. Science fiction focuses on technology. Fantasy focuses on magic.

CHAPTER 1

MAGIC AND MYTHS

Fantasy is a **genre** of fiction. Genre means type. Fantasy is based on magic. There are 2 main types of fantasy.

High fantasy stories are **epics**. Epics are long stories. They're grand. They have heroes. They have **quests**. Quests are journeys. High fantasy has big themes. An example is saving the world. High fantasy often has dragons. It has magicians. It has warriors. It has battles. It has many characters. It has many plots. It has big settings.

Low fantasy is less grand. It's set in the real world. It has magical elements.

Today, many fantasy stories are based on Norse myths, such as ones about the Norse God, Thor, shown here.

Magic is presented in different ways. In some fantasy, magic is through a **portal**. Portals are like doors. These stories have a real world. They also have a fantasy world. Characters go from one to the other. In other fantasy, magic is normal. It's part of everyday life. Some stories feature schools of magic. Some feature creatures living among people. An example is vampire stories.

Some fantasy is inspired by **myths**. Myths are stories. They reflect early history. They reflect cultures. Many myths have fictional beasts. Examples are dragons, giants, and elves.

Fantasy fans have a sense of wonder. They escape into worlds of make-believe.

There are a lot of fantasy stories. Many are battles between good and evil.

CHAPTER 2

THE HISTORY OF MAKE-BELIEVE

Magic and myths are in ancient texts. Ancient means a long time ago. Modern fantasy emerged with George MacDonald (1824–1905). MacDonald was a Scottish author. He wrote *The Princess and the Goblin*. He inspired many fantasy writers. He inspired Lewis Carroll (1832–1898). Carroll wrote *Alice's Adventures in Wonderland*. MacDonald inspired C. S. Lewis (1898–1963). Lewis wrote *The Chronicles of Narnia*. MacDonald inspired J. R. R. Tolkien (1892–1973). Tolkien wrote *The Lord of the Rings*. MacDonald inspired Madeleine L'Engle (1918–2007). L'Engle wrote *A Wrinkle in Time*.

All these authors made fantasy popular. Young readers loved fantasy. Fantasy became connected to children's literature. In the 1990s, fantasy became a big deal again. J. K. Rowling (born 1965) wrote the *Harry Potter* books.

NERD LINGO!

ANCIENTS
Ancients are the source of magic. They made the magic used in fantasy stories. They're the original magicians. They lived a long time ago.

DARK LORD
The Dark Lord is evil. He's the villain. He's a threat. He uses dark magic. He must be defeated.

NECROMANCY
Necromancy is dark magic. It's dangerous. It's focused on mastering death. Magic is used to raise the dead. It's used to extend life. This is unnatural. There's always a price to pay.

SLIMES
Slimes are weak monsters. They're used as jokes. They're not scary. They're often the first to die.

THE CHOSEN ONE
The Chosen One is the hero. The hero restores the natural order of the world.

URBAN FANTASY
Urban fantasy is a genre. These stories are set in city streets. Magic exists as a secret. Only a few people know about it.

Magazines also helped make fantasy popular. In 1923, *Weird Tales* came out. It was the first fantasy magazine. More magazines followed.

Today, many **media franchises** are fantasies. Media franchises are a collection of related media. Fantasy is in books. It's in TV shows. It's in movies. It's in video games. Characters and worlds are connected. An example is the Marvel universe. Marvel has comics. But it also has movies, TV shows, and more. Superhero stories are connected.

Fans love fantasy. They form fan clubs. They go to fan conventions. They dress like their favorite characters They role-play. Fantasy is here to stay.

Fantasy magazines have stories. They have art. They have fan letters.

The Tolkien fandom is huge. These fans are called The Ringers.

CHAPTER 3

IMAGINING THE IMPOSSIBLE

There are different types of fantasy fandoms. One of the most popular is the Tolkien fandom. Tolkien fans love LOTR. LOTR is *The Lord of the Rings*. Fans also love *The Hobbit*. These Tolkien stories are set in Middle-earth. They're about a quest. Hobbits, elves, and humans band together. They seek to save the world. There's a magic ring. There are battles.

The Tolkien fandom started in the 1960s. Fans launched a Tolkien Reading Day. It's a day to celebrate Tolkien's work. This happens on March 25. In the story, evil is defeated on this day.

People also study LOTR. They're called Tolkienists. They study languages used in LOTR. They study family histories.

TOO NERDY!

LEGO makes tiny blocks. These blocks are plastic. They're colorful. They interlock. They connect together. They're used to make many things. A children's museum in China is called Smaerd Land. *Smaerd* is "dreams" spelled backward. It's China's largest indoor children's museum. It has 8 themes. It has a special display. It has a model inspired by *The Lord of the Rings*. The model is set in this fantasy world. It depicts Middle-earth. It has battle scenes. It has forts. It has rivers of lava. It has a big castle. It has soldiers. It has underground caves. It set a world record. It's the largest mini-brick model ever. More than 50 builders worked on it. It took 3 years to make. It uses more than 150 million blocks. It covers more than 2,060 square feet (191 square meters). Fans love it. They see familiar scenes. They see their beloved story come to life.

Another popular fandom is around Disney. Disney fans are all around the world. Fans go to Disney parks. They dress as Disney characters. They watch Disney content. They collect Disney items. Disneyana refers to Disney **collectibles**. Collectibles are things collected as a hobby. The Disneyana Fan Club was formed in 1984. It has about 30 chapters, or subgroups.

Many of Disney's stories use magic. They're based on fairy tales. They have talking animals. They have catchy songs. They have happy endings.

Disney fans are of all ages. Adult fans are called Disney Adults. Some Disney Adults host Disney-themed weddings. They're extreme fans.

Walt Disney (1901–1966) made popular cartoons. He created the Disney brand.

Potterheads are Harry Potter fans. This fandom is huge. It's called Pottermania. Rowling's Harry Potter is a wizard. He goes to Hogwarts. Hogwarts is a magic school. Potter battles a dark wizard.

There are many Potterhead activities. There are **fansites**. Fansites are websites. One site sorts fans into houses. Hogwarts students in the books are sorted into four houses. Each house has its own history. It has its own traits. Fans like feeling connected to the stories.

Potterheads have formed rock bands. They created "wizard rock." This is music with Harry Potter themes. Band members dress as characters. A band example is Harry and the Potters.

There are musicals. There are games. There are tours and much more.

Potterheads nerd out about visiting The Wizarding World of Harry Potter™ in Florida.

Marvel stories are set in real cities. DC stories are set in make-believe cities. Superman protects the city of Metropolis.

Fans love superheroes. Superheroes have magical powers. They're awesome fighters. They're brave. They're strong. They save the day. They first appeared in comics. Now, they're in movies and TV.

There are 2 main comic companies. DC Comics created Superman and Batman. Marvel Comics created Spider-Man and Captain America. Both companies have many fans. Some fans like to debate which company is better. They compare the superheroes.

Fans tend to have favorite superheroes. They like their costumes. They like their powers. They like their origin stories. Origin stories are characters' backgrounds. They explain characters' actions. They explain their thinking.

Shang-Chi is a Marvel superhero. He is the master of **kung fu**. Kung fu is a Chinese fighting style. In 2021, a movie about Shang-Chi came out. The movie used **wuxia**-style fighting. It inspired American fans.

Wuxia is a genre of Chinese fantasy. It's about the quests of fighters. It takes place in ancient China. Fighting skills are extreme. They're at superhuman levels. Wuxia fighters can fly in the air. They can jump large spans. They can run across water. They can jump over high walls.

Wuxia excites fans. It's beautiful to watch. It's also packed with action.

Simu Liu (born 1989) played Shang-Chi.

NERD TO KNOW!

Chadwick Boseman (1976–2020) was an actor. He was a Black American. He starred as Black Panther. This gave him international fame. Black Panther was a Black superhero. He's part of the Marvel universe. Most superheroes are White. Boseman was the first Black actor to lead a Marvel movie. This is a big deal. Boseman said, "There's a hero here that I hope people grow to love." Black Panther first appeared in comics in 1966. His name is T'Challa. He rules Wakanda. Wakanda is a fictional African nation. It has advanced tech. It has ancient power. Black Panther has magical strength. He's a warrior. He's a scientist. He's rich. He has high-tech tools. He's the first major Black superhero in American comics. This character led the way for other Black superheroes. Boseman said, "To be young, gifted, and Black...we know what it's like to be told that there's not a screen for you to be featured on. We knew we had something special that we wanted to give the world."

Online forums are message boards. Fans can message each other.

CHAPTER 4

RELEASE YOUR INNER NERD

You, too, can be a fantasy nerd! Try one of these activities!

JOIN AN ONLINE GROUP!

Fantasy books can be hard to read. There are many details. There are new settings. There may be strange names and words. All this can be unfamiliar to readers.

Readers may be confused. Joining online groups can help. Ask questions. Fans can give answers. They can help explain things. They can discuss ideas. Many fans are online. This lets you hear different viewpoints.

Think about making your own fansite. Create your own online group. Make sure to state the rules. Make sure to be active.

HOST A MOVIE MARATHON!

Marathons are long events. Movie marathons involve watching many movies in a row. People watch one movie after another. They watch them on the same day. They take little or no breaks.

Many fantasy stories are long. They're a **series**. Series are a set of related stories. There are several movies in a series. Gather some fantasy fans. Host a movie night. Binge-watch a fantasy series. **Binge-watch** means to watch movies or shows all at once.

Doing this may help you track the story better. It'll be easier to remember the characters. It'll be easier to remember the plots.

Fairy tales are fantasy. Many, like *Cinderella*, have been turned into movies.

BUILD A FANTASY WORLD!

Good fantasy writers focus on **world-building**. This means they create strong settings. They create **lore**. Lore includes history and traditions.

Writers build worlds for their characters. They create what the world looks like. They create what the world feels like. They create what the world sounds like. They create the world's history.

Create rules. Think about magic. Think about how it works. Think about how people interact. The world needs to make sense. It needs to be the same throughout the story.

Include diversity. Having different characters is good. It makes stories more interesting.

There are many fantasy writers. Most are inspired by the real world.

NERDY TIPS!

TIP #1

FANTASY FANS SUSPEND BELIEF. THIS MEANS THEY PAUSE REALITY. THEY KNOW MAGIC ISN'T REAL. BUT THEY CHOOSE TO BELIEVE IN MAGIC. THEY DON'T QUESTION IT. THEY GO WITH THE FLOW. ALLOW YOURSELF TO ENJOY FANTASY. LET YOURSELF BELIEVE IN WHIMSY.

TIP #2

MANY FANTASY STORIES HAVE A LOT OF CHARACTERS. CHARACTERS ARE FROM DIFFERENT FAMILIES. THIS MAKES READING FANTASY HARD. IT'S HARD TO KEEP TRACK. WRITE NOTES. CREATE A CHARACTER GUIDE. MAKE FAMILY TREES.

TIP #3

SOME FANTASY STORIES ARE LONG. TAKE YOUR TIME. GO SLOW. ENJOY THE JOURNEY. LEARN ABOUT THE WORLD. LEARN ABOUT THE CHARACTERS. DON'T RUSH THROUGH THE STORIES.

TIP #4

SOME FANTASY STORIES HAVE INVENTED LANGUAGES. LEARN TO SPEAK ONE OF THESE LANGUAGES. SOME EXAMPLES ARE ELVISH LANGUAGES. ELVISH LANGUAGES ARE FROM *THE LORD OF THE RINGS*. THERE ARE SOME ELVISH LANGUAGES CREATED BY OTHER PEOPLE, TOO. SPEAK ELVISH WITH OTHER FANS. IT CAN BE LIKE A SECRET LANGUAGE.

GLOSSARY

ancient (AYN-shuhnt) from a time long ago

binge-watch (BINJ-wawch) to watch movies or shows all at once, one after another

collectibles (kuh-LEK-tuh-buhlz) items valued and sought by collectors

conventions (kuhn-VEN-shuhnz) large meetings of fans who come together to talk about and to learn more about a shared interest

epics (EH-piks) long stories, usually about a hero's journey

expos (EK-spohz) large public exhibitions

fandoms (FAN-duhmz) communities of fans; combines "fanatic" and "kingdom"

fansites (FAN-sietz) websites created and maintained by fans about a specific topic or celebrity

genre (ZHAHN-ruh) a category, type, or style of artistic composition

kung fu (KUHNG FOO) a Chinese martial arts style

lore (LOHR) a body of traditions and knowledge on a subject

marathons (MAIR-uh-thahnz) long events

media franchises (MEE-dee-uh FRAN-chyz-ez) a collection of related media including books, TV, movies, and video games

myths (MITHS) traditional stories of an early people that reflect cultural understandings and worldviews

origin stories (OR-uh-juhn STOR-eez) the backgrounds or histories of characters

portal (POR-tuhl) a door or gateway

quests (KWESTS) adventures or journeys

series (SEER-eez) a number of similar or related events or related media programs, one following another

world-building (WERLD-bil-ding) the process of developing a detailed and plausible fictional world for a story

wuxia (WOO-see-ah) a genre of Chinese fantasy fiction about the adventures of martial artists with supernatural abilities in ancient China

LEARN MORE

Loh-Hagan, Virginia. *T is for Thor: A Norse Mythology Alphabet.* Ann Arbor, MI: Sleeping Bear Press, 2020.

Ratcliffe, Amy. *A Kid's Guide to Fandom: Exploring Fan-Fic, Cosplay, Gaming, Podcasting, and More in the Geek World!* New York: Running Press Kids, 2021.

Rowling, J. K. *The Harry Potter Wizarding Almanac: The Official Magical Companion to J. K. Rowling's Harry Potter Books.* New York: Scholastic, 2023.

INDEX